THE

JOYS

OF MOTHERHOOD

THE

JOYS

OF MOTHERHOOD

JANE HUGHES PAULSON

STARK BOOKS
**Andrews McMeel
Publishing**
Kansas City

01 02 03 04 05 BIN 10 9 8 7 6 5 4 3 2 1

Library of Congress Cataloging-in-Publication Data
Paulson, Jane Hughes.
  The joys of motherhood / Jane Hughes Paulson.
    p. cm.
  ISBN: 0-7407-1412-0 (pbk.)
    1. Motherhood—Miscellanea. I. Title.
HQ759 .P33 2001
306.874'3—dc21   00-045005

Book design by Holly Camerlinck

────────────── **Attention: Schools and Businesses** ──────────────

Andrews McMeel books are available at quantity discounts with bulk purchase
for educational, business, or sales promotional use. For information, please write to:
Special Sales Department, Andrews McMeel Publishing, 4520 Main Street,
Kansas City, Missouri 64111.

For my greatest joys,
Jay, Robert, and Christopher

INTRODUCTION

I tell my kids I'm lucky. I always wanted to be a
mother, and they've made it possible. I feel luckier
still to be writing about something so dear to my
heart, the joy of motherhood. When I began
gathering notes for this book, I became more and
more excited as I remembered all the fun, and
important things, hard lessons, and revelations that
make being a mother so remarkable.

I love having children. I remember waking up
each day after my first son was born, with a sense of
anticipation I can liken only to what I feel on
Christmas morning. I'd hurry to his crib, and there
he would be smiling up at me. When I was expecting

my second baby I wondered, as I watched my firstborn playing in the sandbox, how I could ever love another child as much. It didn't seem possible. The baby arrived and in no time established his place in the universe and in my heart. And so it was with my third son.

The best part of being a mother for me is getting to see the world through my children's eyes. And the advice I offer every mom is to take the time to enjoy it. Be conscious of how you spend your time, especially with your child. It's harder than it sounds. Try not to do two or three things at once. I hate it when I go to bed and can't remember what I did all day. Pay attention, I'm forever reminding myself.

No matter where you are on the journey, a mother to be, new mom, or veteran mom, you'll never do anything more important or more meaningful. Be grateful. Your children will get the message. If you sometimes doubt it's getting through, you can always tell them how lucky they make you feel.

THE

JOYS

OF MOTHERHOOD

Hearing the words "You're going to be
a mother" for the first time

A chance to do everything different from
the way your mother did

Eating for two: Be sure to get

enough calcium, protein, fiber, and iron,

drink plenty of water, and exercise.

Feeling your baby move inside you

Holding your newborn in the
delivery room

A helpful and loving husband/partner

Your baby's major firsts:

smile, laugh, tooth, step, word

Reading to your children:

You can't start too early. Even infants

like the sturdy board books. Besides

being great for teething, when you read,

the cuddling, the sound of your voice,

and the colorful illustrations are all

pleasant for your baby, and you are

establishing a pattern of reading

for life.

The sound of your kids making you
breakfast in bed

Mother's Day!

Mom.com and all those other great
mom Web sites: The truth is out there!

Hearing your baby say, "Ma Ma!"

The Mother–Daughter Tea

Picnics! You can never go on too many picnics with your kids. They don't have to be elaborate. Peanut-butter-and-jelly sandwiches on a quilt under the tree in the backyard taste just as good as deviled eggs and fried chicken from a wicker hamper in the park. Frankly, my boys preferred the peanut butter! Take a Frisbee and the dog if you've got one.

Teaching your son to do the box step

Watching your husband wrestling
with the kids on the bedroom floor

Making something everybody likes
for dinner

Being a soccer mom

Hearing your baby's heartbeat in utero

Seeing your child graduate from college

Having your three-year-old pick you
a flower—hopefully not one of your
neighbor's prize zinnias!

A mother's arms are made of

tenderness, and children sleep

soundly in them.

—*Victor Hugo*

Watching your five-year-old blow out
the candles on her birthday cake
all by herself

Family day at the zoo

Having answers to all your child's
questions for a few years at least

Planting a garden with your kids: If you don't have a yard, you can do great things in containers, pots, and half barrels. You can grow vegetables or flowers. If you don't want to use containers, my kids loved growing alfalfa sprouts in a mayonnaise jar. They grow fast, which kids like, and you can throw them in salads or put them on sandwiches. Just don't expect your kids to eat them!

THE

JOYS

OF MOTHERHOOD

Helping your child learn to read when she's ready: Let her set the pace, don't push.

The day your son's feet
are bigger than yours

Hearing yourself be quoted by
your child as an authority—who cares
on what subject

Watching your child learn how to ride a bike: It took me three children to figure out that learning to ride a bike on the sidewalk was crazy. My husband and I took our youngest to a deserted parking lot, where he could wiggle and wobble and ride in circles until he really got the "balance" thing. It made such an amazing difference not to have to learn to ride down a straight ribbon of cement!

Doting grandparents

❧

Being able to "make it all better"

❧

Having kids who can program the VCR

Pizza night! My sister Susie inaugurated this idea. Once a week, usually Friday night, her family orders pizza. Everyone looks forward to it, especially my sister!

Your daughter modeling her first pair of high heels

Being relieved of two heavy bags of groceries by your fourteen-year-old son

Watching cartoons with your kids on
Saturday morning in your bathrobe

A baby who takes long naps

Making chocolate chip cookies with
your kids and eating a lot
of the dough

Your toddler's bath time with lots

of safe bubbles and plenty of toys:

rubber duckies, boats, you name it!

The tooth fairy

Watching your kids sleep, then
tiptoeing downstairs to have a cup
of decaf with your husband

THE

JOYS

OF MOTHERHOOD

Her children rise up

and call her blessed.

—*Proverbs 31:28*

The sock monster: It's the only logical explanation why, when two of your son's socks go into the washing machine, only one comes out.

THE

JOYS

OF MOTHERHOOD

Helping your kids with their homework

Being able to understand the homework

Knowing a good tutor if your child
gets stuck with a subject you can't
figure out together

Teaching your children to

be compassionate: I read recently

that empathy is considered the most

important component of a person's

emotional intelligence. This can

determine success in life.

Think about it.

Hearing your child say thank you
without being reminded

Going shopping with your daughter
for her first bra

Reading the funny paper out loud
to your kids

Mentors: It's reassuring

as your children get older to see them

guided in their deepest interests

by models you both can admire.

Listening to your mother tell
your daughter stories about things
you did when you were a little girl

Playing in the leaves with your kids

Your child's first day of school:
Be sure to take lots of pictures,
and maybe some Kleenex.

Teaching your fifteen-year-old son
to drive

Surviving the driving lessons

Helping your daughter
plan her wedding

THE
JOYS
OF MOTHERHOOD

Breast-feeding your baby: It's not for everyone, but it's great for the baby and mom, too, if she can manage. When my first son was born, I thought I could just pick him up and away we'd go on this peak experience. I soon learned otherwise. It takes about six weeks for a mother and her newborn to become a "nursing couple." Don't be put off. Whatever time you have to give to this unique experience is special time, being with your child in an extraordinary way.

Packing for summer camp: Be sure
to hide a few surprises in with the
clothes: a new deck of playing cards,
or a tin of those fancy French fruit
drops. I also tuck in a little "love"
note along with some writing paper
and several prestamped,
preaddressed envelopes home.

THE
JOYS
OF MOTHERHOOD

Letters from your eleven-year-old son

at camp, especially the ones saying

he misses your food

Disposable diapers!

Your kids in bed with you,
your husband, and the dog on a
lazy Sunday morning

All women become like their

mothers. That is their tragedy.

No man does. That is his.

—*Oscar Wilde*

Chasing after the ice cream man
and catching him

🌹

Hearing your child say he loves you

🌹

Running with your seven-year-old
daughter on the beach

Doll hospitals: If your child's favorite doll or stuffed toy is damaged, don't despair. Professional help is available at the Doll Hospital in Spring, Texas, (281) 350-6722, or Antie Clare's Doll Hospital in North St. Paul, Minnesota, (651) 770-7522. Clare notes that frequently it is the family dog causing the damage. She wisely suggests introducing dolls and stuffed animals to your pet as if the toys are extended family. Repairs can get pricey depending on what's required, but then, it *is* surgery! For additional facilities, check your local listings, or go on-line.

THE

JOYS

OF MOTHERHOOD

The way the world changes when you have a child: Movies, books, songs— everything is different. You have a new worldview as a mother.

Eating a melting Fudgsicle with

your kids: Lick fast!

THE

JOYS

OF MOTHERHOOD

Family hugs

Being able to find whatever is lost . . .
most of the time

Listening to your child's dreams

Letting it be all right to make a mess:

Do your part to stamp out

perfectionism!

Watching your baby eat Cheerios
one tiny *o* at a time

Helping your kids learn to
set boundaries

Letting your kids put
makeup on you

Phonics

Sharing your values
with your children

Teaching your kids about money:
What they learn from you will have
an important influence on them as
adults, so take time delivering
the message.

Glow-in-the-dark, stick-on stars:

Let your kids put them up, or get in on

it yourself—big dippers, smiley faces—

the sky is literally the limit! I used to

forget the stars were on the ceiling in

my son's room. When I'd turn off the

light after kissing him good night,

what a surprise!

Braiding your daughter's hair

French-braiding your daughter's hair

Dancing with your son at his wedding

The future destiny of the child

is always the work of the mother.

—*Napoleon Bonaparte*

Being compassionate with your child:
It's difficult always to respond from the
heart, especially during a disagreement,
and particularly when you have a
teenager who knows how to push
your buttons. If you make responding
compassionately a goal for yourself,

trying to keep your child's point of view

in mind, you'll succeed more often than

not. You'll probably be drawn into fewer

arguments, too, because you won't lose

control. I read about this loving and

reasonable approach in *Between Parent

and Teenager* by Dr. Haim G. Ginott.

It helped me.

A dental checkup when your kids
have no cavities

Your three-month-old sleeping
through the night

Buying your baby's layette:
sleepers, booties, tiny t's, the fun stuff

Seeing your child learn to swim

Playing shark in the pool
with your kids

Letting your kids carry you in
a swimming pool: They love it!

Maternal instincts

A rousing card game with your kids:
My favorite game is Slap. Divide a
deck of cards among two to five players.
Each person puts down a card. If two
match, the first person to slap them gets
the cards. Repeat. Sometimes the pile
of cards gets pretty big before there's
a match. Play until one person has
all the cards. Even really little kids
get this one.

Having a tea party with your kids:
Even though I have three boys, they
had a sturdy tea set. We usually just
pretended, but sometimes I'd fill the
pot with apple juice. I'd ask what kind
of tea they were serving, and they'd
make up all sorts of crazy flavors, like
cheeseburger tea. If you've got time,
invite the teddy bears!

Letting your kids bury you
in the sand at the beach

Teaching your child to pray

Listening to your child's prayers

Being mentioned spontaneously
in your child's prayers

Alone time: When my kids were younger, I tried to spend a few minutes alone with each one before he went to sleep. This was often when the real events of the day slipped out. Sometimes there were tears, but mostly there were laughs, hugs, and a bunch of kisses that sent them off to sweet dreams. I really looked forward to these few minutes, and I think my guys did, too.

THE

JOYS

OF MOTHERHOOD

Remembering to take the time to *stop* and really focus on your child's work when she brings home a drawing or spelling test from school to share with you

A long-distance call from your son away at college just to say "hello"

Choosing a name for your baby:

What a responsibility! In some

African tribes a child isn't

considered alive until the newborn

has been named.

Making alphabet soup: quick and easy! Pick up alphabet pasta at the grocery, add it to fresh or canned chicken broth, and simmer for ten minutes. That's it! You can get fancier, but my kids like it simple, no green stuff. It's a fun Saturday special lunch or supper surprise. Keep the pasta till the time is right and then enjoy learning your ABC's all over again.

I really learned it all

from my mother.

—*Dr. Benjamin Spock*

Having a family game night:
Make or buy some brownies, and dig out
the old board games, Monopoly, Clue,
Risk, even checkers! This is a low-cost
activity that gets the laughs going and
the memories forming. Make it a
once-a-month date. If your kids
are older, let them invite friends.

Going through old baby pictures

with your child: Kids love to look at

pictures, reminisce about themselves,

and see you as a younger mom.

A baby staying dry through the night

No more diapers!

The unsolicited words
"Need some help, Mom?"

The terrible twos: They aren't

all that terrible, and on a bad day

remember the words of Solomon—

This too will pass.

THE

JOYS

OF MOTHERHOOD

Kids' songs, tapes, and CDs:
Keep a bunch in your car and be sure
to sing along. There are so many great
ones, from nursery rhyme classics like
"Jack and Jill" and "Mary Had a Little
Lamb" to "Baby Beluga," or choose
selections from shows like *Sesame Street*
and *Barney*. Camp songs and folk tunes
are also good sing-along sources. My
family's favorite is a real oldie, the
"Wabash Cannonball." It's a catchy tune
about a powerful locomotive. The boys
liked imitating the "whoo-whoo" of the
train whistle as we drove around
doing errands.

Your nine-year-old daughter's
ballet recital

Discovering a ladybug with your toddler

For being linked to apple pie

Sharing your cultural heritage
with your kids

THE
JOYS
OF MOTHERHOOD

Playing peek-a-boo with your baby

Going on a train ride with your kids

Sleeping overnight on the train in
one of those neat compartments

The grateful look on your son's face
when you arrive at school with
the lunch he forgot

Taking a bubble bath after

the kids have gone to bed:

Light a scented candle.

Taking your seven-year-old

for a ride in a swan boat in the

Boston Public Garden: Read Robert

McCloskey's wonderful picture book

Make Way for Ducklings first.

Going to the circus with your kids

Having a teacher or other parent tell you
what nice manners your son has

Home videos: Keep a tape in your camera and try to pull it out several times a year, not just for birthdays and Christmas. Be sure to label the tapes so they don't get taped over! I instituted an "archive" box for the safekeeping of family memory tapes. My kids know if a tape is in that box it gets white-glove treatment and has to be returned to the box after viewing. It works . . . most of the time.

Attending a classroom birthday celebration for your child: If you can't bake cupcakes, pick up donuts, or make Rice Krispies Treats. Kids love them, and they're a lot faster than baking. One year my middle son asked for miniature lemon meringue pies! I couldn't refuse such an original request or resist the challenge. They turned out very tasty.

A mother understands

what a child does not say.

—*Jewish proverb*

Watching clouds with your child:

There's nothing more relaxing

than deciphering shapes from

a cloud-filled sky.

Family vacation: It's not a
contradiction in terms. My fondest
memories of growing up are of long
car trips, motel pools, and lots of
diner fried chicken. When else
do you have access to your parents
and siblings 24/7?

Splashing in puddles after it rains:
Let the kids come too!

Watching your six-year-old son run up
the slide on the playground

Keeping a photo album of your kids as
they hurl themselves through childhood

Baby swings in the park

TV moms: Being connected to such
an American icon isn't so bad.

Getting your ten-year-old
daughter a kitten

Letting your kids play in the sprinklers

Bambi: It means more when
you're a mom.

Keeping a journal: I am forever encouraging my friends to keep journals. As with exercise, it's never too late to start. Get a pretty blank book or spiral notebook, or keep your journal electronically. There is no better way to remember the details of the time that is whirling by. You don't need to be a good writer, just put down your thoughts, the moments in the day that were good or bad. Three, or thirty,

years from now, you'll have forgotten

how, when your oldest was five, he

brought you a caterpillar. You put it in

a jam jar while he ate dinner, then helped

him let it go before bed. It will come

back to you in your journal, sweet and

satisfying. This is a good activity for

kids, too. Start them early on a

rewarding habit.

Annual school pictures of your kids:

You'll buy them even when they're lousy.

They're worth it for the embarrassing

moments they'll provide later.

Watching your daughter climb a tree

Playing tag with your kids: My favorite
is freeze tag with no tag backs.

Getting over an argument with your teen

THE

JOYS

OF MOTHERHOOD

Star-gazing with your kids

on the hood of the car:

It's even better in the desert!

Watching your husband teach your son
how to tie a necktie.

Walking hand in hand with your
three-year-old who talks constantly

When love is gone,

there's always justice.

And when justice is gone,

there's always force.

And when force is gone,

there's always Mom.

—*Laurie Anderson*

Hearing the words "It's sprained not broken" as the emergency room doctor pats your in-line-skating son on the back.

Being asked for advice by your seventeen-year-old daughter

Seeing your kids building a snowman, especially if you are snug inside!

Sonograms of your unborn baby

Hiking with your kids

Watching your baby go barefoot
in thick grass

Going barefoot with your baby!

Cook's night off: Once a week,

once a month, whatever you can swing.

THE

JOYS

OF MOTHERHOOD

Blowing bubbles with your kids: My favorite bubble brew is Pustefix. It's made in Germany and comes in a dark blue tube with a bubble-blowing bear on the front. It's thick and makes wonderful rainbow-colored bubbles. I usually find it in smaller, independent toy stores, and I stock up. You never know when you may need the lift only a bubble-blowing session can give you . . . not to mention the kids!

Half birthdays: Just for fun I celebrate half birthdays, nothing elaborate, maybe a special "toast" at dinner or a favorite dessert. The biggest hit was when I made half a birthday cake and decorated it with half the correct number of candles.

Celebrations: Try to make the little victories count, too. Missing only one on a spelling test, being made a crossing guard at school, or making a goal at the soccer game. Dedicate a pretty plate as the plate of honor. The honoree gets dinner served on it. Life is short.

Celebrate!

Rainbows: Try following one

to the end. Take your kids!

A Christmas gift your child bought
for you with his own money

Buying hair ribbons for your daughter

Going to the park to feed the ducks:

We always took day-old bread.

Unlike my kids, the ducks really

liked the crusts!

Mother Earth: I like being identified with such a commanding archetype.

The eyes in the back of your head: Your kids know they're there, too!

The certificate that says your child is on the Honor Roll at school

Flying kites: Why make the kids wait

for the March wind? Find a hilltop

or beach and send a kite soaring!

Helping your son make his Pinewood
Derby racing car for Cub Scouts

Watching your son's car win the
Pinewood Derby: It *could* happen!

All that I am or ever hope to be

I owe to my angel Mother.

—*Abraham Lincoln*

Bicycling with your kids:
Wear helmets, of course!

Your child's fever going down
after a long, hot night

The pink stuff, good old amoxicillin

Letting everyone make himself what he wants for dinner. At my house we call this foraging, and it's always a big hit with my guys. They have been known to ask for it. Mom, can we forage tonight? You may want to set a few ground rules, for instance, everyone has to clean up after himself, too!

Kid archives: Save those letters from camp, report cards, valentines, drawings, et cetera in a transfile. I have one for each child, the kind you keep tax records in. You can get them at an office supply store. They have lids and are stackable. Give the files to your kids when they finally get their own places. They'll be glad to have them.

Getting as much sleep as you can:
The world is a lot cheerier after a
good night's sleep. When possible
take to your bed!

Finding out what you thought
your child was up to is not as bad
as you thought

Stopping for a few minutes to
watch the sunset with your family

Playing patty-cake with your baby:

They get it earlier than you expect.

Sledding downhill with your son
who thought you were too chicken
to do it, and loving it.

Chewable vitamins

Seeing your five-year-old tie his shoes
by himself

Giving away your maternity clothes

🌺

Being there when your child says,
"Can I ask you something?" and you
know it's been really worrying him.

🌺

Hearing your children reminisce
about their childhoods when they're
only fourteen!

Surviving sibling rivalry:

Every parent should read the book

Siblings Without Rivalry by Adele Faber

and Elaine Mazlish.

Movie night: Dedicate an evening regularly, and take turns picking at the video store. This is a relaxing, family-centered activity. During the week you can talk about the film.

Baby-size Mary Janes

A license to snoop *discreetly*: If they
leave it out or in a pocket that's going
into the wash, hey, they had their
chance to get rid of the evidence!

Breast pumps

Mothers all want their sons

to grow up to be president,

but they don't want them

to become politicians

in the process.

—*John Fitzgerald Kennedy*

Smoke detectors: You'll sleep better once you have them. Check the batteries regularly, too. The days we change to and from daylight saving time each spring and fall are good times to replace them.

A great rocking chair

❀

Making a family tree with your kids

❀

Juice boxes

❀

Wishing on a shooting star in your
backyard with your seven-year-old

THE

JOYS

OF MOTHERHOOD

Grandparents' day at your children's school: There is something very satisfying about your children sharing what they do all day with your and/or your husband's parents.

Teaching your kids how to set the dinner table: I don't know how many times I've said, "The fork goes on the left," but I believe someday my children will thank me.

Hearing your teenage daughter come in
after her big date

Hearing about the big date

Family myths and legends:

My great-grandfather dreamed his

dead father visited him and warned him

not to go to work in the mine the

next day. My great-grandfather risked

losing his job but stayed home the

following morning. There was

a disastrous cave-in at the mine.

Good story!

Watching the snails after it rains
with your five-year-old son

Playpens

Children who chew with their
mouths shut

Dental sealants

Mother Nature: Another powerful "mother" icon to be identified with, why not?

A butterfly kiss from your six-year-old: That means fluttering your eyelashes against someone's cheek.

Making up silly kisses with your

six-year-old: We had a lot of

different ones—the Eskimo, of course,

we rubbed noses; and the Zombie,

keep your face expressionless and

press unpuckered lips against the

recipient's cheek. The boys loved

that one.

The college fund you started
when your daughter was born

❦

Fluoride! If it's not in your local water,
ask your pediatrician or dentist for
chewable tablets. It really helps
protect teeth.

❦

Potty training: They all get it . . .
eventually!

All mothers have intuition.

The great ones have radar.

—*Cathy Guisewite*

Going on dates with your husband:
We had a standing baby-sitter
Saturday nights when the boys were
little. Sometimes we'd go to a movie
or out to dinner, sometimes we just
went for coffee or shopping. It was
our private time, and we looked forward
to it. I think the kids liked it, too.

THE

JOYS

OF MOTHERHOOD

Teaching your son to sew on a button

Short lines at Disneyland

Having your kids wear seat belts
whenever they ride in a car

Going through some of your
grandmother's things with your kids
and sharing memories of her when
you were a kid

Buying no item that says
"dry clean only"

Hand shadows: Remember the bunny?
How about the elephant?
Ask *your* mother.

Playing Barbies with your
eight-year-old daughter

THE
JOYS
OF MOTHERHOOD

Baby fever: You admire babies in grocery carts, linger in front of kids' clothing stores, and find new meaning in the Pampers ads. The thermometer may read 98.6, but you've got baby fever. If you have a child, you're craving another. If you're childless, your biological clock is working overtime.

Epidurals!

Pull-on disposable training pants

Acting surprised when your child
tells you something you already know

Taking your kids to a
major league baseball game

Eating peanuts and hot dogs with
your kids at a major league baseball game

Knowing your kids cover their mouths
when they sneeze: I personally thank
every parent who promotes this one!

Baby bathtubs: You have a lot more control in a small plastic tub than in your big tub, and your kitchen sink can be dangerous, especially if your dishwasher is running. Hot water backs up into the sink!

Accentuating the positive:

When my kids do something right,

setting the dinner table after only being

asked once, for example, I like to

reinforce their good behavior with a

sincere "Thanks, that really made

getting dinner easier for me."

Knowing best

Bouncy seats: Babies love 'em
and Mom has free hands!

MADD—Mothers Against Drunk
Driving: Because of these moms the
streets are safer for your loved ones.

Rewards, prizes, bribery:
still great motivators

A call from your rarely seen older
neighbor saying the sound of your son's
skateboard is . . . music to her ears! It
reminds her of when her own boys were
young. This really happened! I was so
grateful I sent over a hunk of the lasagna
I was making. She was so grateful, we've
become *real* neighbors.

Baby swings

You too, my mother,

read my rhymes

For love of unforgotten times,

And you may chance

to hear once more

The little feet along the floor.

—*Robert Louis Stevenson*

Baby showers

Sports strollers: The heavy-duty,
three-wheeled deals you can jog with.
Maybe you'll get one at your
baby shower.

Your son's bar mitzvah

Your daughter's bat mitzvah

Hand sanitizers

Family reunions

Showing your child the hospital
where he was born

Catching lightning bugs with your
little ones at dusk on a summer evening
and letting them go

THE
JOYS
OF MOTHERHOOD

Dinosaurs: You might as well get interested if you've got boys. Girls like them, too. Give in, they're fascinating, really!

Mobiles: Hang one over the crib.
Babies three months and up find them
very stimulating.

Getting away for a romantic weekend
with your husband

Your daughter's Sweet 16 party

A Boy Scout Court of Honor
where your son receives a new rank
or merit badge

Jumping rope with your
nine-year-old daughter

Going to a big aquarium with

your kids: Seattle, Boston, New Orleans,

and Monterey and Long Beach

in California are a few fine examples.

Your kids will go wild. Leave

extra time for the sharks. I'm an

otter lover, myself!

Seeing your child perform in the school
play no matter what part

Laughing a lot

THE

JOYS

OF MOTHERHOOD

Mighty is the force of motherhood!

It transforms all things by its

vital heart, it turns timidity

into fierce courage, and dreadless

defiance into tremulous

submission; it turns

thoughtlessness into foresight

and yet stills all self-denial

into calm content.

—*George Eliot*

The book *Runaway Bunny* by Margaret
Wise Brown: I think it's even more
for moms than for kids, and it
resonates as they get older.

Den mothers: saints with neckerchiefs

Being able to scare away the
boogeyman for your three-year-old

THE

JOYS

OF MOTHERHOOD

Mother lode: I like this association
with a really big strike, a rich vein
of gold or silver.

Bringing good snacks to the
Little League games

Swinging in the park:

I remember my mother teaching me

how to pump my legs so I could go

higher and higher.

Baby-proofing your house: That doesn't

mean only covering the electrical outlets.

Don't forget to put your good things

off limits, that Waterford vase you

got for your wedding, for example.

Hollywood family movies
that are *really* for families

Whale watching: If you've got
the chance, do it! It's a fabulous
family outing.

Teaching your kids to be generous:
Encourage them to do community
service, ask them to donate a portion
of their allowance to the church,
and be a good model.

Your seven-year-old daughter in
her petticoats: Even if they're just
for dress up, what fun, especially
under a poodle skirt.

Really surprising your son
at his surprise party

Hearing your kindergartner
count to one hundred

THE
JOYS
OF MOTHERHOOD

Having your thirteen-year-old son
spontaneously start dancing with you
while you're making dinner

Buying your teenage daughter perfume

Easter outfits

Singing to your kids at bedtime: lullabies, Beatles songs, whatever moves them or you. By the time my kids were school-age, my husband and I were doing the songs from entire Broadway musicals! I think our kids figured out this was a way to stay up later.

Decorating a dollhouse
with your daughter

Knowing your kids are all home safe
and in their own beds

The touch of the earth mother in us all

A mother is not a person

to lean on but a person

to make leaning unnecessary.

—*Dorothy Canfield Fisher*

Helping your kids organize
their lemonade stand

A smart and sensitive pediatrician

Encouraging your child's sense
of curiosity: Ask questions,
explore, be curious yourself.
You'll learn something!

A family cabin or special camping spot to go back to year after year: This is something I remember really loving as a child. It was great to go back to the lake where you built a rock wall the summer before, or to find the Scrabble game right where you left it on the cabin bookshelf. A fixed point to return to gives you a great sense of continuity.

Watching your daughter play checkers
with your dad

Seeing your daughter beat your dad
at checkers when you never have

Showing your kids the ocean
for the first time

Electrical outlet covers: Now you can

get a swivel variety that keeps the

outlet closed even if your baby

genius pulls out the safety plug!

Teaching your kids to recycle:
It's good to be kind to Mother Nature.

Getting a compliment from
your teenage son

Swaying in a hammock with your
eight-year-old daughter on a
lazy summer afternoon

Showing your kids how to listen
for the ocean in a conch shell

A piano recital featuring your kids

Understanding that to your
fifteen-year-old son a shirt with a collar
is the equivalent of formal wear

Playing "Itsy Bitsy Spider" over and
over and *over* with your toddler

Your first Lamaze class

Daddy taking your son
for his first haircut

Family traditions: I wanted to pass on some of the traditions my husband and I had grown up with to our sons, but I also wanted to establish some traditions of our own. For example, breakfast in bed on your birthday, picnicking on the same beach every year for Memorial Day, or a family hike on Thanksgiving. These are memories in the making, and your kids will look forward to them.

Microwave ovens

Hamburger Helper

Bringing your newborn
home from the hospital

As is the mother,

so is her daughter.

—*Ezekiel 16:44*

Being grateful: Acknowledge the good things in your life and be vocal about it. I found that I often complained about the little irritations in my day—the garbage disposal that broke, the knees shredded out of my son's school uniform pants again, or the terrible traffic—while I rarely mentioned the small good things—I didn't get a parking ticket even though the meter ran out, the rosebush I thought was dying got a new shoot, and everyone helped make dinner. I decided to try to give the good stuff equal time. When I remember to do it, the good things usually outnumber the annoying ones, and I feel more content.

Halloween: It's my kids' favorite

holiday, so we go all-out with

jack-o'-lanterns on the front steps,

spiderwebs hanging from the porch light,

and a giant skeleton on the door.

I got a lot of points for learning

how to make them up to look

really gory, too.

Having your son offer to wash your car

Being part of a spiritual community

Sending baby pictures by e-mail

Amniocentesis results
saying everything is fine

Knowing the sex of the baby
before it's born

Not knowing the sex of the baby
before it's born

Read-along book tapes: These are great
for car trips or rainy afternoons.
There are lots of titles. Your child
reads along in the book as the narrator
on the tape reads the story.

Mother's Day coupons: My kids started giving me coupons, like gift certificates, for things such as going for a burger and a movie together, taking a walk around the neighborhood, or visiting an art museum. For me, these are better than perfume or costume jewelry, and they know it. It's always fun to see what they come up with, too.

THE

JOYS

OF MOTHERHOOD

The baby books: My husband and I had quite a library, and it's still growing! Each phase of a child's development brings new challenges, particularly the adolescent and teen years. Luckily, there are a lot of great parenting books to help you. I mention a few in other entries, but two additional favorites are *How to Talk So Kids Will Listen and Listen So Kids Will Talk* by Adele Faber and Elaine Mazlish, and *Get Out of My Life, but First Could You Drive Me and Cheryl to the Mall?: A Parent's Guide to the New Teenager* by Anthony E. Wolf.

Buying birth announcements

❀

Playing a silly game under the blankets
with your toddler at bedtime: My
youngest liked a game I named Storm
at Sea. I'd make wind sounds and
wave the blankets over our heads.
We'd cuddle under the flapping covers.

❀

Maternity leave

Showing your son how to pin on a corsage for his prom date

Viewing old family videos with your kids

Curling up on a porch swing with your kids to watch a summer storm roll in

Going to a natural history museum

with your kids: It's like the zoo

only better, all the animals are out!

Getting your figure back after
the baby is born

Helping your six-year-old
write a letter to Santa

The collections: My middle son
collects snow globes of Christmas
scenes, the Statue of Liberty, a surfer
dude, whatever. We've lost a few, but he
enjoys the ones that survive!

Mother always said that honesty
was the best policy, and money
isn't everything. She was wrong
about other things, too.

—*Gerald Barzan (attr.)*

Hearing the words "It's okay to push"
when you're in labor

The older women in the park
who make a fuss over your baby

Enjoying today: The ladies in the
park are right, it, meaning baby time,
goes fast!

Wet wipes

Playing paper dolls with your
eight-year-old daughter

Planning a tree house with your kids

Getting your husband to build
the tree house

THE

JOYS

OF MOTHERHOOD

Taking your family to see the Grand Canyon: I admit I stayed in the car parked near the rim much of the time with our then four-year-old. I couldn't stand to get any closer with an active preschooler, but my husband and our two older sons hiked down a mile inside the canyon, and we all had fun in the beautiful national park.

Going on every field trip you can:
By middle school you'll be persona
non grata at a lot of activities, so go
while the going is good.

Homemade ice cream:
Now it's your kids' turn to crank,
unless you've gone electric.

Visiting the maternity ward when you are expecting your first baby: I remember how everyone's eyes popped out when they wheeled by a woman in labor on a gurney, and how everyone ogled the newborns in the nursery window.

Looking at your own newborn
through the nursery window
with your husband

Liking your kids' friends

Setting up an aquarium in your seven-year-old's bedroom. The fish are entertaining, and it makes a good night-light. It gives the term "sleeping with the fishes" new meaning.

❧

Taking your kids to your favorite musical

❧

Dr. Spock's Baby and Child Care: Still the best "operator's manual" available

Grocery carts with built-in infant seats

Celebrating the day your son is
taller than you are

The Heimlich maneuver: Know how
to do it and hope you never have to.

THE

JOYS

OF MOTHERHOOD

There is no more important work

than raising the next generation.

This is what mothers do.

—*Alexandra Stoddard*

A set of blocks: Invest in the
heavy-duty, wooden, school-type variety.
They're expensive but worth every penny,
whether you have boys or girls.
(We asked the grandparents to go in
together for a set one Christmas.)
Leave them out and watch your kids
go to block heaven, for years!
Our kids never got tired of them.

THE
JOYS
OF MOTHERHOOD

Getting past the "everything goes
in the mouth" stage

Discovering your son has a girlfriend

Being introduced to your son's girlfriend

Blackout shades: Our middle son is a light sleeper, and the shades bought us more than an hour of early-morning sleep when he was a baby.

Allowance: Establish a set day

of the week for distributing the cash,

then stick to it.

Training your kids to write
thank-you notes: A coach at the end
of the season, for example, or
grandparents who live far away
and have sent a birthday gift will
enjoy receiving a personal thanks.

THE

JOYS

OF MOTHERHOOD

Sharing your beauty secrets
with your daughter

Your baby's laugh

Having a set bedtime for the kids

Sticking to the set bedtime

Taking your family to a fabulous
fireworks display on the Fourth of July

Teaching your child the facts of life
but not telling her more than she
wants to know

Satisfying your own needs: Moms spend a lot of time taking care of everyone else. Don't be a martyr. If you're feeling resentful, you may need to do something special for yourself. Often little things work great for me, a new color nail polish, for example, maybe a manicure. Tell the kids you need twenty minutes alone. They'll get the idea. Do one small thing just for you each day. The effects are cumulative, believe me. You'll feel the difference.

Keeping a baby book: Don't beat

yourself up if you get behind

in your notations. It will give you

a place to stick the birthday cards,

invitations, class pictures, et cetera.

You'll be glad you have it.

Starting a mother-daughter book club
with your ten-year-old

Making your kids' favorite cake

Letting them lick the cake bowl

Mother is the name of God

in the lips and hearts of children.

—*William Makepeace Thackeray*

Packing your suitcase to go to the
hospital to have the baby. Don't forget
to take something for your newborn
to wear home, too.

A really good recent photograph
of your family

Lysol: Don't keep house without it,

especially during flu season.

THE

JOYS

OF MOTHERHOOD

Car safety seats: It's hard to believe

there was a time without them.

Don't forget to bring one

to the hospital to take your

baby home.

Polaroid or digital cameras:

Keep one loaded on the closet shelf.

There is a lot to be said for

instant gratification.

Game Boy

Letting your kids make
instant chocolate pudding

Watching your husband
become a father

The first stage of labor:

It's pure excitement and not

a lot of pain

Taking your child to get a library card: When my youngest son was in second grade, he noticed the Caldecott Medal on a book he was checking out. It's been given each year since 1938 by the American Library Association to the artist of the most distinguished American picture book for children.

My son was intrigued. He liked to draw.

We agreed to read every book that had

won the award. We got a list from the

librarian and checked off the title each

time we finished a book. It took several

months and visits to various libraries. We

read a lot of good books, and the best

part was we did it together.

THE

JOYS

OF MOTHERHOOD

Your kids' jack-in-the-box:

I love it when that little guy pops out.

You think maybe he won't, then he does.

Every time!

Being your kid's biggest fan

Playing jacks with your daughter:
I love to play with a golf ball.

Having a five-year-old who wants
cowboy boots

Diaper Genie: This is a great addition to the nursery. It holds dirty diapers and seals them for "odor control" and disposal.

Cheap socks: Since your

thirteen-year-old son considers socks

appropriate outdoor footwear,

cheap is good.

THE

JOYS

OF MOTHERHOOD

Family camp: This is a great way to spend time together. Family camps have activities for all ages, offering a safe environment to share activities you might not normally get to. Get out of your regular routine and have someone else do the cooking!

The trust in your child's eyes

Ant farms

Starting a charm bracelet for your
eleven-year-old daughter

I was a better mother

before I had kids.

—*Lori Borgman*

Being a blood donor: You can help save

a life and set a good example for your

kids by giving back to your community

in this very special way.

Going after the blanket: No one will sleep if your toddler's "lovey" is lost. It's irreplaceable. Our youngest son left his "green blanket" appropriately in Ireland. He was almost four, so I figured I'd just wean him. He was very persistent asking about it, however, and I finally called the establishment where the blanket was last seen. They had found it, rag that it was, and were happy to mail it on to us. It arrived a week later smelling of scones. The look on our son's face when he saw it has stayed with me.

Lycra! There's nothing like it
for post-baby stomach control.

Letting your kids solve some of
their own problems

Finding out your kids are pretty good
at problem solving

A *hot* cup of coffee

THE

JOYS

OF MOTHERHOOD

Writing to your daughter while she's away at college: In this age of electronics, I have it on good authority that it's still great to get good old-fashioned mail.

Family mealtime: Make this a special

part of the day whether you're having

turkey or takeout.

Getting rid of the bully:

Nothing restores a mom's peace of mind

better than knowing the class bully has

been confronted, has changed,

or is moving!

Seeing your seven-year-old daughter
let go of her helium balloon
and watching it sail away together

Being an authority figure

Cell phones! Here are my tips for usage: Wear a headset to protect your brain, don't phone and drive, and remember how obnoxious it is to have to listen to people on their cell phones in public.

A good-looking baby bag
that holds everything

Guardian angels

The freckles on your
eight-year-old's nose

Your thirteen-year-old son cleaning up after himself in the kitchen: It might never happen, but it would be a joy!

Trusting your kids

Play dates

Listening a lot: Hold the lecture.

Going to a photo booth and
hamming it up with your kids

Mother-daughter look-alike outfits:

Go ahead, just a few times when

she's little, for fun!

By and large, mothers and housewives are the only workers who do not have regular time off. They are the great vacationless class.

—*Anne Morrow Lindbergh*

Playing charades with your kids

The dimple in your son's right cheek

Taking your kids to a puppet show

Helping your kids put on
their own puppet show

Buying a nice string of pearls for your daughter's twenty-first birthday: These are a classic, and they don't have to cost a fortune. Jackie Kennedy immortalized a triple strand of faux pearls.

Being there when your kid
hits a home run

Giving your kids a sense of adventure

Pancake breakfasts: Enjoy someone

else's cooking for a good cause!

We often drop in on local celebrations

while on vacation. It's an inexpensive

way to feed the family, and you get in

on local color at the same time!

Family code words: We used to have

neighbors, the Krauses, who read

their Sunday paper on the patio

in their bathrobes. For us that

seemed the ultimate in relaxation,

so in our family "krausing" became

synonymous with taking it easy.

Knowing your child is old enough
to cross the street by herself

Participating in the Ms. Foundation
for Women's annual Take Our Daughters
to Work Day

THE
JOYS
OF MOTHERHOOD

Nurturing the offspring

of your son's horned lizard:

This could mean having to buy

live baby crickets somewhere.

Making up an impromptu scavenger hunt for your kids: Give them a paper sack and a list of ten things they can find around the neighborhood, and off they'll go. Make sure you've got a little prize for the winner, and something else for the runners-up, ice cream bars, some quarters for the video arcade, whatever your kids are into.

Play groups

A child who can entertain himself
on Saturday morning without getting
into trouble, so you can sleep in

Framing your third-grader's self-portrait

The plaster mold of your
five-year-old's little hand

🌹

Baby-sitting co-ops

🌹

A good nail brush next to the
soap dish for serious hand washing

🌹

Knowing where your first-aid kit is
in an emergency

The hand that rocks the cradle

Is the hand that rules the world.

—*William Ross Wallace*

Buying a crib for your baby

❧

Knowing how to discipline your kids
so it works

❧

Baby carriers: slings, front packs,
and backpacks

Turning off the TV: Some families discover themselves when the TV is silent. Moderation has always been the point I strive for, so I hold no extreme views, TV or not TV. We had a house rule that there was TV after school for the kids' "prime time" between 3:30 and 5:00 P.M., then it went off for the evening to do homework and have dinner. We were loose about weekend viewing, but thanks to sports and friends, TV has never become an addiction for our kids.

Staying up too late gabbing
with your college-age daughter
and her friends

Naming a guardian for your child:
You don't want to leave this most
important decision to the state.

Your baby's toes

Playing "This Little Piggy Went to Market" with your baby's toes

Taking your three-year-old for his

first ride on a merry-go-round:

One of my favorites is a handsome

old-timer near the beach in Watch Hill,

Rhode Island. It even has a brass ring!

THE

JOYS

OF MOTHERHOOD

Animal crackers: low-fat, low-cal,

and they taste great with tea!

Kids like them, too.

Letting your kids bury their parakeet
in the backyard: Children enjoy rituals.
A pet funeral is an opportunity to
say good-bye formally, and a chance
for you to gently discuss a most
important aspect of life, death.

THE

JOYS

OF MOTHERHOOD

Your child being
"student of the month"

An afternoon to yourself
while your husband takes the kids
to the park

Knowing CPR: For even more peace of mind, if your kids are old enough, organize a workshop at their school; then they'll know it, too.

THE
JOYS
OF MOTHERHOOD

Saying yes: It's fun to keep them guessing. Say yes sometimes when your kids think you'll say no. I don't mean being arbitrary, but you can tell by the way they phrase the question. I can't go swimming before dinner, can I?

Driving the middle school car pool:
Keep your mouth shut and they'll forget
you're there. Then you'll get an earful!

THE

JOYS

OF MOTHERHOOD

Trusting your twenty-one- and
eighteen-year-old sons to stay home
while you and your husband take
a second honeymoon for two weeks

Coming home after trusting your
twenty-one- and eighteen-year-old sons
with your home for two weeks to find it
still standing, clean, and with no
complaints about loud parties from
the neighbors

A big toy box

Immunizations!

Baby massage

Picking your battles

with your teenager: It's great not to

fall into every trap that's set!

The relationship to the mother is

the first and most intense.

—*Sigmund Freud*

THE

JOYS

OF MOTHERHOOD

Teaching your kids to clean up

after themselves: At least trying to

teach them!

Riding in the front car of the roller

coaster with your ten-year-old son:

He'll be really impressed.

THE

JOYS

OF MOTHERHOOD

Making a will or living trust with

your husband: You'll be glad you did.

Your kids spending the weekend with grandparents: This is a special opportunity for everyone. The kids get spoiled, the parents get some alone time, and the grandparents get to give the kids back at the end of the weekend.

THE
JOYS
OF MOTHERHOOD

Swimsuit diaper disposables:

As a former lifeguard, I can tell you

this is a great development.

The lock on the bathroom door

Eating the crusts off your kids'
peanut-butter-and-jelly sandwiches

You and your husband walking down
the aisle with your daughter at
her wedding

THE
JOYS
OF MOTHERHOOD

Weaning your baby

Keeping a drawer or box filled
with old costumes, masks, hats,
capes, scarves, et cetera—bring it out
on a rainy day

Kid-friendly restaurants:

Real restaurants, the ones with a

children's menu and sometimes even

crayons to color on the white-paper

table covers. My favorite is a small

Italian cucina that offers a ball of pizza

dough for kids to sculpt while Mom

and Dad relax with a glass of wine.

Bravissimo!

Riding a Ferris wheel with your kids:

I like getting stuck at the top

for a little while.

Being caught by your kids dancing
with your husband in the living room

Your new baby's adorable naked body

In-ear thermometers

Spill-proof sipper cups

THE
JOYS
OF MOTHERHOOD

Hearing a professional storyteller with your kids: Libraries and bookstores often offer this kind of event. A good storyteller can bring a story to life. She might even be an inspiration to a reluctant reader.

Crayons: The "quiet toys" I think they call them. Keep lots of scrap paper handy, and you've got time for an uninterrupted phone call!

For that's what a woman,
a mother, wants—to teach her
children to take an interest
in life.

—*Marguerite Duras*

Girl Scout cookie time: Moms get

a lot of credit for helping coordinate

and distribute all those yummy cookies!

It's worth the effort when you see

how proud your daughter is of

her achievement.

Figuring out how to keep a low profile and still be a presence in your teenagers' lives: That's quite a balancing act! They need you. They just don't want to know you exist.

Starting a scrapbook
with your daughter

Mother Goose

Microwave popcorn!

Staying up late to watch scary movies with your eleven-year-old son: Be sure to make lots of popcorn! Despite all today's fast-action and gory movies, most kids love the classic horror flicks, *Dracula, Frankenstein, King Kong,* especially if there's mom-time involved.

Knowing help is out there if your child
has a problem you and your husband
can't help her with

Not being afraid or ashamed to get
help if your child needs it

A good tickle attack: My kids used to love it when I made my hand into the "tickle machine" and it went briefly out of control. Try your own version, or feel free to use mine! It's guaranteed fun and laughs.

Putting your children to bed on
Christmas Eve

Bragging about your kids—a little
sometimes when they can hear you

Building a blanket fort with your
six-year-old

A child's rocking chair: This was a very popular item with our oldest, especially when his brother came along. He pulled his little rocker right next to mine, and we rocked his brother together.

School fairs where they give away goldfish in plastic bags: There's something so Norman Rockwell about these events—bakery booths and ringtoss—I love them!

THE
JOYS
OF MOTHERHOOD

Going to the drive-in movie with
your kids in their pajamas

Seeing your husband and son
setting up a model railroad

Gymboree!

Your daughter's call saying
she got "there" safely

Flash cards: Addition, subtraction,

or multiplication tables, they're a

math reality check in a box.

A house full of your son's friends:

They might make a mess, but you know

where they are.

A mother's hardest to forgive.

Life is the fruit she longs

to hand you,

Ripe on a plate. And while

you live,

Relentlessly she understands you.

—*Phyllis McGinley*

Car trips: Take snacks, drinks, and lots of tapes or CDs of kid stories and songs. Teach your kids to read maps; discuss the geography and history of the places you visit. Make up games. I grew up in the Midwest, and our favorite car game was, believe it or not, called Cow.

The passenger side of the car competes with the driver's side. Each team counts the cows in the fields on their side. The team counting one hundred cows first wins. Pass a cemetery on your side and lose all your cows. My mother invented another car game called Mouse. There is only one rule: The first person who talks loses. Pretty smart!

Volunteering at a food pantry
with your teenager

Lego toys

Discovering your fifteen-year-old
daughter made her bed without
being asked

When your kids get along and
really enjoy each other

Showing your kids the house
where you grew up

Your baby wearing your
great-grandmother's baptismal gown

Newbery Medal books: Annually since 1922, the American Library Association has awarded the Newbery Medal for the most distinguished American children's book published the previous year. *Johnny Tremain, A Wrinkle in Time,* and *Island of the Blue Dolphins* are three of my favorites. All the winning titles are in print, and many are in paperback. Ask your bookseller or librarian about these terrific books, or visit the ALA web site for a complete list.

Letting him keep the stray: If you can't make a permanent commitment, at least until you can place it yourself, or find a humane shelter.

Pacifiers: Don't leave home without one!

Twins, double the pleasure

Being ready to go back to work after the baby is born

Helping your ten-year-old daughter get
ready to have her first slumber party

Your baby's smile

Wall fairies: My mother could knock gently on any wall in our house, and magically, when she opened her closed hand, there would be a fistful of jelly beans or licorice bits! We asked where the candy came from, and she told us it was from the fairies that lived in the wall. The fairies only visited when we were very, very good (and when my mother had candy), because they were shy and hated noise, and messes. I continued this game with my own children with similar pleasing results.

The excitement of moving into a bigger
house so the family can spread out

Active or "open" listening

The look of gratitude on your child's
face when you apologize to her for a
misjudgment or a mistake

Getting over morning sickness

Your husband telling you you're beautiful
when you're nine months pregnant and
weigh more than he does

Knox Blocks: Tough, extra-thick

gelatin cubes babies can play with

or eat, or both!

The most important thing a father

can do for his children is to love

their mother.

—*Theodore Hesburgh*

The alphabet song: Who can resist

a five-year-old's prideful rendition

of this timeless classic?

Sending a care package to your son

in college: He still goes for your

chocolate chip cookies.

Understanding it's better to be

your child's mom than her best friend:

She can make friends, but she's got

only one mom.

THE

JOYS

OF MOTHERHOOD

Letting your kids make mistakes

Bunk beds

Good friends who send over a
delicious casserole when you
come home with your new baby

Nursery monitors

Walking the dog your son promised to
take care of, if you'd only let him
keep it

Helping the kids fete Dad big time
on Father's Day

When your kids see you're blue
and try to cheer you up

Sunscreen: for them and for you

Baby shampoo

"Mommy and me" class

Baby shampoo

A reliable baby-sitter your kids like, too

Family meetings: Once a week, after dinner for example, take a few minutes as a family to review upcoming events, soccer games, business trips, overnights, and birthday parties. Everyone will gain from the prior notice. We keep a family calendar on the refrigerator with all significant dates logged in.

Other moms

Homemade Mother's Day gifts

A spontaneous kiss from your child,
whatever age

Showing your firstborn to your mother